NEIL T. ANDERSON

YOUR
IDENTITY
IN
CHRIST

HARVEST HOUSE PUBLISHERS
EUGENE, OREGON

Cover design by Bryce Williamson

Cover photo © Elisabeth Schittenhelm, vovik_mar / Getty Images

Interior design by Chad Dougherty

For bulk, special sales, or ministry purchases, please call 1-800-547-8979. Email: Customerservice@hhpbooks.com

Your Identity in Christ

Taken from *The Bondage Breaker*®
Copyright © 2007, 2019 by Neil T. Anderson
Published by Harvest House Publishers
Eugene, Oregon 97408
www.harvesthousepublishers.com

ISBN 978-0-7369-8624-3 (pbk)
ISBN 978-0-7369-8625-0 (eBook)

Printed in the United States of America

22 23 24 25 26 27 28 29 30 / BP / 10 9 8 7 6 5 4 3 2 1

CONTENTS

CHAPTER ONE

YOU HAVE EVERY RIGHT TO BE FREE

Lydia was a middle-aged woman who was dealt a bad hand. Memories of ritual and sexual abuse that she suffered as a young child had haunted her throughout her life. Her shattered self-perception was written all over her when she came to see me. As Lydia told me her story, she displayed little emotion, but her words reflected total despair.

"Lydia, who do you think you are? I mean, how do you perceive yourself?" I asked.

"I think I'm evil," she answered stoically. "I'm just no good for anybody. People tell me I'm evil, and all I do is bring trouble."

"As a child of God, you're not evil. You may have done evil things, but at the core of your very being is a desire to do what is right, or you wouldn't be here," I argued. I handed her the following list of scriptures describing who she is in Christ:

—————————— IN CHRIST ——————————

I am accepted:

- John 1:12   I am God's child
- John 15:15   I am Christ's friend
- Romans 5:1   I have been justified
- 1 Corinthians 6:17   I am united with the
                         Lord and one with Him
                         in spirit
- 1 Corinthians 6:20   I have been bought with
                         a price—I belong to God
- 1 Corinthians 12:27   I am a member of
                         Christ's body
- Ephesians 1:1   I am a saint
- Ephesians 1:5   I have been adopted as
                         God's child
- Ephesians 2:18   I have direct access to
                         God through the Holy
                         Spirit
- Colossians 1:14   I have been redeemed
                         and forgiven of all my
                         sins
- Colossians 2:10   I am complete in Christ

I am secure:

- Romans 8:1-2   I am free from condemnation

- Romans 8:28   I am assured that all things work together for good

- Romans 8:31-34   I am free from any condemning charges against me

- Romans 8:35-39   I cannot be separated from the love of God

- 2 Corinthians 1:21-22   I have been established, anointed, and sealed by God

- Colossians 3:3   I am hidden with Christ in God

- Philippians 1:6   I am confident the good work God has begun in me will be perfected

- Philippians 3:20   I am a citizen of heaven

- 2 Timothy 1:7   I have not been given a spirit of fear but of power, love, and a sound mind

- Hebrews 4:16   I can find grace and mercy in time of need

- 1 John 5:18   I am born of God and the evil one cannot touch me

I am significant:

- Matthew 5:13   I am the salt and light of the earth

- John 15:1-5   I am a branch of the true vine, a channel of His life

- John 15:16   I have been chosen and appointed to bear fruit

- Acts 1:8   I am a personal witness of Christ

- 1 Corinthians 3:16   I am God's temple

- 2 Corinthians 5:17-20   I am a minister of reconciliation

- 2 Corinthians 6:1   I am God's coworker

- Ephesians 2:6   I am seated with Christ in the heavenly realm

- Ephesians 2:10   I am God's workmanship

- Ephesians 3:12   I may approach God
                          with freedom and
                          confidence

- Philippians 4:13   I can do all things
                          through Christ, who
                          strengthens me

"Would you read these statements out loud right now?" I asked. Lydia took the list and tried the first one: "I am G-G-God's ch-ch…" Suddenly her whole demeanor changed, and she sneered, "No way, you dirty *bleep*!"

It is never pleasant to see the evil one reveal his ugly presence through a victim like Lydia. I calmly exercised Christ's authority and shared with Lydia about her identity in Christ. Realizing that she was not just a product of her past, but rather, a new creation in Christ, she was able to throw off the chains of spiritual bondage and begin living according to who she really was, a child of God.

Later, Lydia told me that when I asked her to read the list, it appeared to go blank. Satan didn't want her to know the truth of who she was in Christ or how Jesus meets her needs for life, identity, acceptance, security, and significance. He knew that God's truth would disarm his lie just as surely as light dispels darkness.

You Are a Child of God

Nothing is more foundational to your freedom from

Satan's bondage than understanding and affirming what God has done for you in Christ and who you are as His child. Your attitudes, actions, responses, and reactions to life's circumstances are greatly affected by what you believe about yourself. If you see yourself as a helpless victim of Satan and his schemes, you will probably live like a victim and be in bondage to his lies. But if you see yourself as a dearly loved and accepted child of God, you will likely start living like one. That is what John said in 1 John 3:1-3: "See how great a love the Father has bestowed on us, that we would be called children of God; and such we are…Beloved, now we are children of God…and everyone who has this hope fixed on Him purifies himself, just as He is pure."

Every defeated Christian I have worked with has had one thing in common. None of them knew who they were in Christ nor understood what it means to be a child of God. Scripture is very clear: "As many as received Him, to them He gave the right to become children of God" (John 1:12). "The Spirit Himself bears witness with our spirit that we are children of God, and if children, heirs also, heirs of God and fellow heirs with Christ…so that we may also be glorified with Him" (Romans 8:16-17). Our identity and position in Christ is not only the basis for living a liberated life in Christ, but the foundation upon which we minister to others. We can't impart to others what we don't possess ourselves.

You Are Spiritually and Therefore Eternally Alive

God created us to have a material self and an immaterial self, or an outer nature and an inner nature (2 Corinthians 4:16). The material self is your physical body, and the immaterial self is your soul/spirit. Because we are created in the image of God, we have the ability to think, feel, and choose (the combination of mind, emotions, and will are usually identified as the soul), and the ability to relate to God (if we are spiritually alive). As a Christian, your soul/spirit comes into union with God at the moment of your conversion, and that makes you spiritually alive. (Note: I use the terminology *soul/spirit* because conservative theologians don't unanimously agree about whether the human soul and spirit are the same or separate entities.)

As a believer, you are no longer "in Adam," you are "in Christ." Because the life of Christ is eternal, the spiritual life you now have in Christ is eternal. Eternal life is not something you get when you die physically; you receive it the moment you are born again! "He who has the Son has the life; he who does not have the Son of God does not have the life" (1 John 5:12).

Contrary to what Satan would like you to believe, he can't separate you from God, who has promised to never leave you nor forsake you (Hebrews 13:5). You don't have to physically die to get rid of tormenting spirits, which is a lie that deceived people commonly believe. You can submit to God and resist the devil, and he will flee from you (James 4:7).

You Are a New Creation in Christ

If you don't fully understand your identity and position in Christ, you will likely believe there is little distinction between yourself and nonbelievers. Every verse in the list at the beginning of the chapter is true about every believer, and none of the verses are true about the natural person. The accuser will seize that opportunity, pour on the guilt, and question your salvation if you don't know who you are. Defeated Christians confess their sins and strive to do better, but inwardly they think, *I'm just a sinner saved by grace, hanging on until the rapture. Having my sins forgiven was the only thing that happened at salvation. I am still the same person I was before.*

Read how Paul describes who you were *before* you came to Christ: "You were dead in your trespasses and sins, in which you formerly walked according to the course of this world, according to the prince of the power of the air...and were by nature children of wrath" (Ephesians 2:1-3). As a believer you have become a partaker "of the divine nature, having escaped the corruption that is in the world by lust" (2 Peter 1:4).

As a born-again child of God, you are no longer "in the flesh"; you are now "in Christ." "You are not in the flesh but in the Spirit" (Romans 8:9). "You were formerly darkness, but now you are light in the Lord; walk as children of light" (Ephesians 5:8). "From now on we recognize no one according to the flesh…If anyone is in Christ, he is a new creature" (2 Corinthians 5:16-17). Paul doesn't identify believers by their flesh patterns. We are not alcoholics, addicts, codependents, pedophiles, or victims. We may struggle with some of those flesh patterns, but that is not who we are.

The New Testament refers to the person you were before you received Christ as your old self (old man). At salvation, your old self, which was motivated to live independent of God and was therefore characterized by sin, died (Romans 6:6); and your new self, united with Christ, came to life (Galatians 2:20). Because your soul is in union with God, you are identified with Him:

- In His death (Romans 6:3; Galatians 2:20; Colossians 3:1-3)

- In His burial (Romans 6:4)

- In His resurrection (Romans 6:5,8,11)

- In His ascension (Ephesians 2:6)

- In His life (Romans 5:10-11)

- In His power (Ephesians 1:19-20)

- In His inheritance (Romans 8:16-17; Ephesians 1:11-12)

Your old self had to die in order to sever your relationship with sin, which dominated it. Being a child of God doesn't mean that you are sinless (1 John 1:8). But because your old self has been crucified and buried with Christ, you no longer *have* to sin (1 John 2:1). You sin when you choose to believe a lie or act independently of God.

You Can Be Victorious over Sin and Death

Death is the end of a relationship, not the end of existence. Sin is still a reality, and appealing, but the power and authority it had over you has been broken. "Therefore there is now no condemnation for those who are *in Christ Jesus*. For the law of the Spirit of life *in Christ Jesus* has set you free from the law of sin and of death" (Romans 8:1-2). The law of sin and the law of death are still present, and that is why Paul used the word "law." You cannot do away with a law, but you can overcome it with a greater law, which is the "law of the Spirit of life in Christ Jesus."

Furthermore, flesh patterns are still present. Although you are no longer *in the flesh* as your old self was—you are now *in Christ*—you can still choose to *live according to the flesh* (Romans 8:12-13), complying with those old urges that were conditioned to respond independently of God.

Paul teaches that God the Father "made Him who knew no sin to be sin on our behalf, so that we might become the righteousness of God *in Him*" (2 Corinthians 5:21). When Jesus died on the cross, our sins were placed on Him. But when He rose from the grave, there was no sin on Him. When He ascended to the Father, there was no sin on Him. And today, as He sits at the Father's right hand, there is no sin on Him. Because we are seated in the heavenlies, alive in Christ, we too have died to sin.

When we find a promise in the Bible, the only appropriate response is to claim it. When we find a commandment in Scripture, we should obey it. And when the Bible tells us the truth about who we already are and what Christ has already done, such as in Romans 6:1-10, there is only one appropriate response: to believe it.

Christ has already died to sin, and because you are in Him, you also have died to sin. You cannot do for yourself what Christ has already done for you. Notice the use of the past tense in Romans 6:1-10:

- "We who *died* to sin" (verse 2)

- "All of us who *have been baptized* into Christ Jesus *have been baptized* into His death" (verse 3)

- "We *have been buried* with Him" (verse 4)

- "Our old self *was crucified* with Him, in order that our body of sin might be done away with, that we should no longer be slaves to sin" (verse 6)

- "For he who *has died* is freed from sin" (verse 7)

- "If we *have died* with Christ, we believe that we shall also live with Him" (verse 8)

The verbs in these verses indicate what is already true about us because of what Christ has done for us. The only right response is to believe.

We have a responsibility as well: "Even so consider yourselves to be dead to sin, but alive to God in Christ Jesus" (verse 11). Paul uses a present-tense verb because we are to continuously believe this truth. Believing it doesn't make it true—it is true whether we believe it or not. You may not feel dead to sin, but you are to *consider* it so because it *is* so. Some ask, "What experience must I have for this to be true?" The only necessary experience is that of Christ on the cross, which has already happened; and the only way to appropriate that truth is to believe it. Others try to put the old self to death and can't because the old self has already been crucified.

We don't make anything true by our experiences. Rather, we are to choose to believe what God says is true, then live accordingly by faith. Then the truth works out in our experience. It is not what we do that determines who we are; who we are determines what we do. We don't labor in the vineyard hoping that God may one day accept us. God has already accepted us, and that is why we labor in the vineyard.

We can't do what Christ has already done for us, but

we have to assume our responsibility to keep ourselves from sinning. Paul tells us how, in Romans 6:12-13: "Do not let sin reign in your mortal body so that you obey its lusts, and do not go on presenting the members of your body to sin as instruments of unrighteousness; but present yourselves to God as those alive from the dead, and your members as instruments of righteousness to God." You are dead to sin, but you can still serve it by putting your body at sin's disposal. It's up to you to choose whether you're going to use your body, which includes your brain, for sin or for the sake of righteousness.

Because of Christ's victory over sin, you are free to choose not to sin. It is your responsibility to not let sin reign in your mortal body. That is why the apostle Paul wrote, "I urge you therefore, brethren, by the mercies of God, to present your bodies a living and holy sacrifice, acceptable to God, which is your spiritual service of worship" (Romans 12:1).

For example, if you commit a sexual sin, you have used your body as an instrument of unrighteousness, and consequently, you have allowed sin to reign in your mortal body. Simple confession probably will not resolve the conflict. But a person can pray, asking God to reveal to their mind every sexual use of their body as an instrument of unrighteousness, and God does. He usually starts with their first experience and works forward. As He brings those experiences to mind, the person is encouraged to renounce that use of their body; ask God to break the spiritual, mental, and emotional bond between themselves and anyone with whom they may have committed a sexual sin; and finally, give their body to God as a living sacrifice. Then they can be transformed by the renewing of their mind (Romans 12:2).

You Can Be Free from the Power of Sin

If you have allowed sin to reign in your mortal body, you know how hard the battle is. I've faced it myself. So did the apostle Paul. In Romans 7:15-25, he wrote about struggling with the same feelings of frustration. This passage clearly shows that the law is incapable of setting us free. I believe it also reveals what the struggle is like when we allow sin to reign in our mortal bodies. (Some believe this passage refers to Paul's preconversion experience. I disagree because every disposition of Paul's heart in this passage is toward God. In addition, the natural man does not "joyfully concur with the law of God" [verse 22] and "[confess] that the Law is good" [verse 16].)

I invite you to listen in as I walk through this passage with Dan, who had been struggling to overcome the power of sin in his life:

Neil: Dan, let's look at a passage of Scripture that seems to describe what you're presently experiencing. Romans 7:15 reads, "What I am doing, I do not understand; for I am not practicing what I would like to do, but I am doing the very thing I hate." Would you say that this verse describes you?

Dan: Exactly! I desire to do what God says is right, but sometimes I find myself doing just the opposite.

Neil: You probably identify with verse 16 as well: "If I do the very thing I do not want to do, I agree with the Law, confessing that the Law is good." How many personalities or players are mentioned in this verse?

Dan: There's only one person, and it is clearly "I."

Neil: It's very defeating when we know what we want to do, but for some reason can't do it. How have you tried to resolve this in your own mind?

Dan: Sometimes I wonder if I'm even a Christian. It seems to work for others, but not for me. Often I wonder if the Christian life is even possible.

Neil: If you and God were the only players in this scenario, it would stand to reason that you would either blame God or yourself for your predicament. But look at verse 17: "So now, no longer am I the one doing it, but sin which dwells in me." How many players are there now?

Dan: Apparently two, but I don't understand.

Neil: Let's read verse 18 to make some sense out of it: "I know that nothing good dwells in me, that is, in my flesh; for the willing is present in me, but the doing of the good is not."

Dan: I know that I'm no good.

Neil: That's not what it says, Dan. In fact, it says the opposite. *Whatever it is that is dwelling in you is not you.* If I had a splinter in my finger, it would be "nothing good" dwelling in me. But the "nothing good" isn't me; it's the splinter. It's also important to note that this "nothing good" is not even my flesh—it is dwelling *in* my flesh.

If we saw only ourselves in this struggle, it would be hopeless to live righteously. These passages are going to great lengths to tell us that there is a second party involved in our sin struggles whose nature is different from ours.

You see, Dan, when you and I were born, we were born under the *penalty* of sin. And we know that Satan and his emissaries are always working to keep us under that penalty. When God saved us, Satan lost that battle, but he didn't pull in his fangs. He is now committed to keeping us under the *power* of sin. We also know that he is going to work through the flesh, which remains with us after salvation.

Let's read on to see how this battle is being waged: "The good that I want, I do not do; but I practice the very evil that I do not want. But if I am doing the very thing I do not want, I am no longer the one doing it, but sin which dwells in me. I find then the principle that evil is present in me, the one who wishes to do good" (verses 19-21).

Dan, can you identify from these passages the nature of that "nothing good" that indwells you?

Dan: Sure, it is clearly evil and sin. But isn't it just my own sin? When I sin I feel so guilty.

Neil: There's no question that you and I sin, but we are not "sin." Evil is present in us, but we are not evil per se. This doesn't excuse us from sinning, however, because Paul wrote earlier that it is our responsibility to not let sin reign in our mortal bodies (Romans 6:12). Do you ever feel so defeated that you want to strike out at someone or yourself?

Dan: Almost every day!

Neil: But when you cool down, do you again entertain thoughts that are in line with who you are in Christ?

Dan: Always, and then I feel terrible about lashing out.

Neil: Verse 22 explains this cycle: "I joyfully concur with the law of God in the inner man." When we act out of character with who we really are, the

Holy Spirit immediately brings conviction because of our union with God, and we often take it out on ourselves. But soon our true nature expresses itself again and we are drawn back to God. It's like the frustrated wife who announces that she's had it with her husband. She wants out and couldn't care less about the bum. But after she acknowledges her pain, she softens and says, "I really do love him, and I don't want a divorce. I just don't see any other way out." That's the inner person, the true self, being expressed.

Verse 23 describes the nature of this battle with sin: "I see a different law in the members of my body, waging war against the law of my mind and making me a prisoner of the law of sin which is in my members." According to this passage, Dan, where is the battle being fought?

Dan: It appears to be in the mind.

Neil: That's precisely where the battle rages. Now if Satan can get you to think you are the only one in the battle, you will get down on either yourself or God when you sin. Let me put it this way: Suppose there is a talking dog on the other side of a closed door and the dog is saying, "Come on, let me in. You know you want to. You will get away with it. After all, who would know?" So you open the door, and the dog comes in and clamps his teeth around your leg. On the other side of the door, the dog plays the role of the tempter, but once you let the dog in, he plays the role of the accuser. "You opened the door! You opened the door!" And what do you do?

Dan: I usually end up confessing because I feel so guilty. But in my struggle with sin, nobody has ever told me about this tempting and accusing dog! I usually end up beating on myself.

Neil: I think you should beat on the dog. On the other hand, just beating on the dog is not enough either. You were right to confess to God, which means you agreed with Him that you did open the door, but confession is only the first step in repentance. Christians who only do that get caught up in the sin-confess-sin-confess-sin-confess cycle and eventually give up. Once they get tired of beating on themselves, they walk away from God under a cloud of defeat and condemnation.

You submitted to God when you confessed that you opened the door; now you should resist the devil, and he will flee from you (James 4:7). Finally, go back and close the door and don't get suckered into opening it again. Repentance isn't complete until you have truly changed.

Paul expressed this feeling of unresolved conflict in verse 24: "Wretched man that I am! Who will set me free from the body of this death?" Note he did not say, *"Wicked or sinful* man that I am"; he said, *"Miserable* man that I am." There is nobody more miserable than the person who knows what is right and wants to do what is right, but his attempts to do the right thing are met with defeat. He wonders, *Is there any victory?*

The answer is in verse 25: "Thanks be to God through Jesus Christ our Lord! So then, on the one hand I myself with my mind am serving the law of God, but on the other, with my flesh the law of sin." Now let's read Romans chapter 8 and see how Paul overcomes the law of sin by the law of life in Christ Jesus.

Dan: I think I'm getting the picture. I've been feeling guilty for my inability to live the Christian life without really understanding how to live it. I've tried to overcome this sin by myself, and I've never really understood the battle for my mind.

Neil: You're on the right track. Condemning yourself won't help because there is no condemnation for those who are in Christ Jesus (Romans 8:1-2). Let's see if we can resolve your conflict with genuine repentance and faith in God. Then we can talk about how to win that battle for your mind and walk by faith in the power of the Holy Spirit. Then you will not carry out the desires of your flesh (Galatians 5:16).

CHAPTER TWO

YOU CAN WIN THE BATTLE FOR YOUR MIND

H e rescued us from the domain of darkness, and transferred us to the kingdom of His beloved Son, in whom we have redemption, the forgiveness of sins" (Colossians 1:13-14).

"If anyone is in Christ, he is a new creature; the old things passed away; behold, new things have come" (2 Corinthians 5:17).

"You have died and your life is hidden with Christ in God" (Colossians 3:3).

If those verses are true, then how come I still struggle with the same thoughts and feelings I did before I became a Christian? I suspect that every honest Christian has at least thought about that question. There is a very logical reason why you still think, feel, and too often act as you did before you were born again.

Mental Strongholds

During your formative years, you had neither the presence of God in your life nor the knowledge of His ways. Consequently, you learned to live independently of God. This learned independence is a major characteristic of what Scripture calls the flesh.

You also learned many mentally and emotionally unhealthy ways to cope with life. Psychologists refer to these unhealthy patterns as defense mechanisms. For instance, if you got in trouble, or thought you would, for telling the truth, you probably learned to lie to protect yourself. Other common defense mechanisms include

- denial (conscious or subconscious refusal to face the truth)

- fantasy (escaping from the real world)

- emotional insulation (withdrawing to avoid rejection)

- regression (reverting to less-threatening times)

- displacement (taking out frustrations on others)

- projection (blaming others)

- rationalization (making excuses for poor behavior)

Defense mechanisms are similar to what Paul called "fortresses," or "strongholds" (NIV). He wrote, "Though we walk in the flesh, we do not war according to the flesh, for the weapons of our warfare are not of the flesh, but divinely powerful for the destruction of fortresses. We are destroying speculations and every lofty thing raised up against the knowledge of God, and we are taking every thought captive to the obedience of Christ" (2 Corinthians 10:3-5).

Strongholds are fleshly thought patterns that were programmed into your mind when you learned to live independently of God. Your worldview was shaped by the environment you were raised in. But when you became a Christian, nobody pressed the CLEAR button. Your old fleshly patterns of thought weren't erased.

If you have been trained wrong, can you be retrained? If you believed a lie, can you renounce that lie and choose to believe the truth? That's what repentance is: a change of mind. We are transformed by the renewing of our minds. That is possible because "we have the mind of Christ" (1 Corinthians 2:16), and the Holy Spirit will lead us into all truth.

Satan's Schemes

The good news is that we can reprogram our minds, but we still need to check for "viruses." Satan's strategy is to infiltrate your mind with his thoughts and to promote his lie in the face of God's truth. If he can control your thoughts, he can control your life. That is why Paul continued in the present tense with the statement, "And we are taking every thought captive to the obedience of Christ" (2 Corinthians 10:5). In this passage, the word "thought" is the Greek word *noema*. How Paul used this word elsewhere in the second letter to the Corinthian church is very revealing.

Paul instructed the church to forgive an offender after they had carried out church discipline "so that no advantage would be taken of us by Satan, for we are not ignorant of his schemes" (2 Corinthians 2:11). "Schemes" comes from the same root word, *noema*. Satan takes advantage of those who will not forgive. After helping thousands find their freedom in Christ, I can testify that unforgiveness is the major reason people remain in bondage to the past.

Concerning evangelism, Paul wrote, "If our gospel is veiled, it is veiled to those who are perishing, in whose case the god of this world has blinded the minds [*noema*] of the unbelieving so that they might not see the light of the gospel of the glory of Christ, who is the image of God" (2 Corinthians 4:3-4). How are we going to reach this world for Christ if Satan has blinded the minds of unbelievers? The answer is prayer.

Paul wrote, "I am afraid that, as the serpent deceived Eve by his craftiness, your minds [*noema*] will be led astray from the simplicity and purity of devotion to Christ"

(2 Corinthians 11:3). My conversation with a 55-year-old undergraduate student illustrates how a mind could be led astray. Jay came into my office one day and said, "Dr. Anderson, I'm in trouble."

"What's the problem, Jay?"

"When I sit down to study, I get prickly sensations all over my body, my arms involuntarily rise, my vision gets blurry, and I can't concentrate. If this keeps up, I'm going to flunk all my classes. I can't even read my Bible."

"Tell me about your walk with God," I probed.

"I have a very close walk with God," Jay boasted.

"What do you mean by that?" I asked.

"Well, when I leave school at noon each day, I ask God where He wants me to go for lunch. If Burger King comes to mind, I go to Burger King. At the counter I ask God what He wants me to eat. If the thought comes to order a Whopper, I order a Whopper."

"What about your church attendance?" I continued.

"I go every Sunday wherever God tells me to go. For the past three Sundays, God has told me to go to a Mormon church."

Jay sincerely wanted to do what God desired for him to do, but he was being deceived. Jay was listening to his own subjective thoughts as if they were God's voice instead of "taking every thought captive to the obedience of Christ" (2 Corinthians 10:5). In so doing, he had opened the door to Satan, with the result that his theological studies were being sabotaged. Deceiving thoughts had convinced him that God was preparing him to be one of the two prophets mentioned in the book of Revelation who were slain in the streets of Jerusalem. Jay even tried to convince his college roommate that he was the other prophet! Tears of gratitude flowed from his eyes when he found his freedom and returned to his right mind.

Satan and Our Minds

Scripture teaches that Satan is capable of putting thoughts into our minds. In the Old Testament, we read that "Satan rose up against Israel and incited David to take a census of Israel" (1 Chronicles 21:1 NIV). What's wrong with taking a census? Shouldn't David know how many troops he has for combat? Satan knew that David had a whole heart for God and would not knowingly defy the Lord. The strategy was to get David to put his confidence in his resources rather than God's.

The same David wrote, "A horse is a false hope for victory" (Psalm 33:17). He knew the battle belonged to the Lord, but suddenly he had this "thought" to take a census against the protests of his military commander, Joab, who knew that to do this was sin. Tragically, 70,000 men of Israel fell as a result of David's sin.

How did Satan incite David? Did he talk audibly to David? No, these were David's thoughts. At least he thought they were. Therein lies the deception. Deceptive thoughts come in such a way (in first person singular) that we think they're our own. I began to realize this years ago while helping others find their freedom in Christ. Thoughts like *I'm stupid, I'm dumb, I'm ugly, I am no good* may be more than "self-talk."

Judas also listened to the devil. "During supper, the devil having already put into the heart of Judas Iscariot, the son of Simon, to betray him…" (John 13:2). We may be tempted to dismiss this as just a bad decision prompted by the flesh, but Scripture clearly says that the origin of those thoughts was Satan.

In Acts 5:3 we're told that Satan filled the heart of Ananias to lie to the Holy Spirit.

Martin Luther wrote, "The Devil throws hideous thoughts into the soul—hatred of God, blasphemy, and despair." Concerning himself he reported,

> When I awake at night, the Devil tarries not to seek me out. He disputes with me and makes me give birth to all kinds of strange thoughts. I think that often the Devil, solely to torment and vex me, wakes me up while I am actually sleeping peacefully. My night time combats are much harder for me than in the day. The Devil understands how to produce arguments that exasperate me. Sometimes he has produced such as to make me doubt whether or not there is a God.[1]

David Powlison, though opposed to the view that demons can invade believers, acknowledges that Satan can put thoughts into one's mind: "'Voices' in the mind are not uncommon: blasphemous mockeries, spurts of temptation to wallow in vile fantasy or behavior, persuasive lines of unbelief. Classic spiritual warfare interprets these as coming from the evil one."[2] Thomas Brooks, in his discussion about Satan's devices, continually spoke of Satan presenting thoughts to the soul of believers.[3]

I have counseled hundreds of believers who were struggling with their thought life. Some have difficulty concentrating and reading their Bible, while others say they hear voices or struggle with accusing and condemning thoughts. With few exceptions, these struggles have proven to be a spiritual battle for their minds. This shouldn't surprise us since we have been warned in 1 Timothy 4:1 (NIV): "The Spirit clearly says that in later times some will abandon the faith and follow deceiving spirits and things taught by demons."

Psychologists and psychiatrists routinely see patients who are hearing voices: chemical imbalance is the standard diagnosis. I believe our body chemistry can get out of balance, and hormonal problems can throw our systems off. But I also believe that other legitimate questions need to be asked, such as, "How can a chemical produce a personality and a thought?" "How can our neurotransmitters involuntarily fire in such ways that they create thoughts that we're opposed to thinking?" Are there natural explanations? We should remain open to any legitimate explanations, but I don't think we will discover comprehensive answers unless we take into account the reality of the spiritual world.

When people say they are hearing voices, what are they actually hearing? The only way we hear audible sounds with our ears is when there is a sound source. Sound waves move from the source through the medium of air and strike our eardrums, sending a signal to our brains. Physically speaking, that is how we hear. But "voices" that people hear or the "thoughts" that they struggle with are not coming from sound sources if others around them are not hearing the same sounds.

Satan and his demons are spiritual beings; they do not have material substance, so we cannot hear them or any spiritual being with our physical ears. "Our struggle is not against *flesh and blood*, but against the rulers, against the authorities, against the powers of this dark world and against the spiritual forces of evil in the heavenly realms" (Ephesians 6:12 NIV).

Brain Versus Mind

There is a fundamental difference between our brains and our minds. Brains are organic matter. When we die physically, we are separated from our bodies, and our brains return to dust. At that moment, we will be absent from our bodies and present with the Lord (2 Corinthians 5:8). But we won't be mindless because our minds are a part of our souls.

Our ability to think is similar to how a computer functions. Both involve two separate components: one is the hardware, which is the actual physical computer (the brain); the other is the software (the mind), which is programmable. A computer is worthless without the software, but neither will the software work if the hardware shuts down.

If something is not functioning correctly between the ears, the medical profession would first consider it to be a hardware problem. If your only reference point is Scripture, you would think otherwise. Of course one can have a neurological problem, or brain damage or dementia. According to Romans 12:1-2, we should submit our bodies to God (which includes our brain), but we are transformed by the renewing of our minds.

After hearing my presentation on this subject, a dear lady wanted some clarification. She said, "I recently visited my daughter on the mission field, and I contracted malaria. I got so sick that I almost died. At the height of my fever, I started to hallucinate. Are you telling me that those hallucinations were demonic?"

"What were you hallucinating about?" I asked.

"Mostly about Pluto, Mickey Mouse, Donald Duck, and Daisy," she replied.

"Did you stop at Disneyland on your way to the mission field?" I inquired, and she responded, "Well yes, I did. How did you know?"

There was nothing demonic about her experience. Her visit to Disneyland was fresh on her mind. When we go to sleep, our physical brains continue to function, but there are "no hands on the keyboard." If you are mentally active and pounding away on the keyboard of your mind, you are not asleep. You go to sleep when you relax and let your thoughts drift. While you are sleeping, your brain continues to function, and it can randomly access whatever has been stored in your memory.

Consider the content of your dreams. Don't they almost always relate to people you know, things you have seen, or places you have been? The stories in your dreams can be rather creative, but the people and places have already been programmed into your memory. Suppose a child watches a horror movie, then goes to sleep and has a nightmare. Chances are the players in the nightmare will be the same ones as in the movie. But when someone has grotesque nightmares with images not previously seen or heard, then I would suspect that the origin is demonic.

The Battle Is Real

We need to expose this spiritual battle for what it is so that we can have a comprehensive answer for those who experience it. Let me illustrate why: What typically happens when frightened children come into their parents' bedroom and say they saw or heard something in their room? One of the parents will probably go look in the child's closet or under the bed, then say, "There's nothing in your room, honey—now go back to sleep!" Yet if you as an adult saw something in *your* room, would you just forget about it and go back to sleep?

Though there never was anything in the room that could be observed by your natural senses, what your child saw or heard was in his or her *mind*, and it was *very real*.

I can't explain the means by which people pay attention to deceitful spirits. Neither do I know how the devil is able to invade our minds, but I don't have to know how he does it in order to protect myself according to Scripture's instructions. The spiritual battle for our minds does not operate according to the laws of nature. No physical barriers confine or restrict the movements of Satan. Yet the frightened face of a child testifies that the battle is real. Why not respond to your child as follows?

"Honey, I believe you saw or heard something. I didn't hear or see anything, so that helps me understand. You may be under a spiritual attack, or you could be having bad memories of something you saw. Sometimes we can't tell the difference between what is real and a dream we just had. Before I pray for your protection, I want you to know that Jesus is much bigger and more powerful than anything you see or hear that frightens you. The Bible teaches us that Jesus, who is living in us, is greater than any monsters in the world. Because Jesus is always with us, we can tell whatever is frightening us to leave in Jesus's name. The Bible tells us to submit to God and resist the devil, and he will flee from us. Can you do that, honey? Let's pray together."

Much of what is being passed off today as mental illness is actually a battle for our minds. Proverbs 23:7 says, "As he thinks within himself, so he is." In other words, you don't do anything without first thinking it. All behavior is the product of what we choose to think or believe. Trying to change behavior without changing what we believe—and therefore what we think—will never produce lasting results.

Because we can't read another person's mind, we have to learn to ask the right questions. Consider the following examples:

Five-year-old Danny was sent to the office of his Christian school for hurting several other children on the playground. He had been acting aggressively toward others and was restless in class. His teacher said, "I'm puzzled by his recent behavior—it isn't like Danny to act this way!" Danny's mother was a teacher at the school. When she asked her son about Jesus, he covered his ears and shouted, "I hate Jesus!" Then he grasped his mother and laughed in a hideous voice!

We asked Danny whether he ever heard voices talking to him in his head. He looked relieved at the question and volunteered that voices were shouting at him on the playground to hurt other kids. The thoughts were so loud that the only way to quiet them was to obey, even though he knew he would get in trouble. We told Danny that he didn't have to listen to the voices anymore. We led Danny through the children's version of The Steps to Freedom[4] and had him pray the prayers along with us. Afterward, we asked him how he felt. A big smile came across his face, and with a sigh of relief, he said, "Much better!" His teacher noticed new calmness in Danny the next day. He did not repeat his aggressive behavior in school.

A committed Christian couple adopted a young boy and received him into their home with open arms. Their innocent little baby turned into a monster before he was five. Their home was in turmoil when I was asked to talk to him. After some friendly chatting, I asked him if it ever seemed like someone was talking to him in his head.

"Yes," he said, "all the time."

"What are they saying?"

"They're telling me that I'm no good."

I then asked him if he had ever invited Jesus into his life. He replied, "Yes, but I didn't mean it."

I told him that if he really did ask Jesus to come into his life, he could tell those voices to leave him. Realizing that, he gave his heart to Christ.

A children's director at a church shared the following testimony, which illustrates the frustration that many face as they try to find the help they need:[5]

My problem began a couple of years ago. I was experiencing terribly demonic nightmares and had nights during which I felt the presence of something or someone in my room. One night I woke up feeling like someone was choking me, and I could not speak or say the name of Jesus. I was terrified.

I sought help from church leaders and pastors. They had no idea how to encourage me. Eventually fear turned into panic anxiety disorder, and my thoughts were so loud, destructive, and frightening that I visited my primary care provider. I thought for sure she would understand my belief that this was a spiritual battle. She responded by diagnosing me with bipolar disorder, and told me that I would be on medication for the rest of my life. She also gave me a prescription for antidepressants and anti-anxiety meds. I was devastated.

I told my husband the diagnosis, and he assured me that it wasn't true. I decided not to take the medication. I just didn't have any peace about doing that. I began Christian counseling, which helped a bit, but when I told my counselor about what was happening in my mind, she too said, "I think it is time for medication."

It seemed like everyone thought I was crazy. No one believed that my problem was spiritual.

Thankfully, I came across one of your books and read stories of people I could relate to. It was in *The Bondage Breaker* that I first heard of The Steps to Freedom in Christ. Going through the Steps was one of the most difficult yet incredible things I've ever done. I experienced a lot of interference, such as a headache and confusion, but having the Holy Spirit reveal to me all that I needed to renounce was incredible. I was amazed by how the Holy Spirit brought out the truth.

After going through the Steps, there were no nagging thoughts. I was totally at peace. I wanted to cry with joy. After that, I wasn't afraid of being alone, and the nightmares were gone. I didn't have to play the radio or television to drown out the terrible thoughts. I could sit in silence and be still.

Taking Every Thought Captive

How do we know whether those negative, lying, and condemning thoughts are from the evil one or just our own flesh patterns? In one sense, it doesn't make any difference. We are to take *every* thought captive to the obedience of Christ. If a thought isn't true, don't believe it. Ask yourself: "Did I want to think that thought or those thoughts? Did I make a conscious decision to think those thoughts?" If not, why do you think those thoughts are yours?

One person laminated a card that she kept with her at all times. The card read, "Where did that thought come from? A loving God?" It *is* possible to know that condemning, blasphemous, and tempting thoughts or voices did not originate from you. On the other hand, you can't tell flesh patterns to leave. They are slowly replaced or overcome as we renew our minds. Paul said we are not to be anxious (double-minded) about anything. Rather we are to turn to God in prayer, "and the peace of God, which surpasses all comprehension, will guard your hearts and your minds [*noema*] in Christ Jesus" (Philippians 4:7). The next verse says we are to let our minds dwell on those things that are true, pure, lovely, and right.

Our relationship with God is personal, and as in any relationship, there are certain issues that have to be resolved in order for the relationship to work. We can't expect God to bless us if we are living in open rebellion against Him. "Rebellion is like the sin of divination, and arrogance like the evil of idolatry" (1 Samuel 15:23 NIV). If we are proud, God is opposed to us (James 4:6). If we are bitter and unwilling to forgive, God will turn us over to the torturers (Matthew 18:34) as a disciplinary effort. These issues have to be resolved first. Then we can experience the peace our Lord purchased for us on the cross.

CHAPTER THREE

JESUS HAS YOU COVERED

C an one ever feel safe living in this fallen world? Consider that question and try to empathize with the woman who wrote the following letter during our weeklong conference Resolving Personal and Spiritual Conflicts:

Dear Dr. Anderson:

I attended your Sunday sessions, but while waiting to talk to you after the Sunday evening meeting I suddenly felt ill. I was burning up like I had a fever, and I got so weak I thought I was going to faint. So I went home.

I need help. I've had more trouble in my life since I became a Christian. I've overdosed on alcohol and drugs so many times I can't count them. I've cut myself several times with razor blades, sometimes very seriously. I have thoughts, feelings, and ideas of suicide weekly, like stabbing myself through the heart. I'm a slave to masturbation; I'm out of control, and I don't know how to stop.

On the outside I appear very normal. I have a good job, and I live with an outstanding family in our community. I even work with junior high students at my church. I can't really explain my relationship with God anymore. I've been seeing a psychiatrist for two years. Sometimes I think I'm this way because of a messed-up childhood, or maybe I was born this way.

How can I tell if my problems are in my mind, or the result of sin and disobedience against God, or the evidence of demonic influence? I would like to talk to you during the conference. But I don't want to try another thing that doesn't work.

Frances

I met with Frances that week, and she was as miserable, frustrated, and defeated as she sounded in her letter. There is a place that we can go and feel safe, but it is not a physical location. Our only sanctuary is "in Christ." Once Frances began to realize that she was not a powerless or defenseless pawn in a spiritual battle, she made choices that changed her situation, and her chains fell off. A year later she wrote,

I was hesitant to write you because I could not believe that my life would be changed or different for any length of time. I'm the girl who tried to kill herself, cut herself, and destroy herself in every possible way. I never believed that the pain in my mind and soul would ever leave so that I could be a consistent and productive servant of the Lord Jesus Christ.

I have given it more than a year, and it was the best year I've ever had. I have grown in so many different ways since the conference. I feel stable and free because I understand the spiritual battle going on for my life. Things come back at me sometimes, but I know how to get rid of them right away.

God's Protection

Wouldn't it be great if every Christian knew "how to get rid of them right away"? If we understood the spiritual battle and knew the protection we have in Christ, there wouldn't be so many casualties.

Satan's first goal is to blind the minds of unbelievers (2 Corinthians 4:3-4). But the battle doesn't stop when you become a Christian. He is still committed to fouling up your life and "proving" that Christianity doesn't work, that God's Word isn't true, and that nothing changed when you were born again.

Some Christians are a little paranoid about evil

powers lurking around every corner looking for someone to devour. That's an unfounded fear. Your relationship to demonic powers in the spiritual realm is a lot like your relationship to germs in the physical realm. You know that germs are all around you: in the air, in the water, in your food, in other people, and even in you. Should you live in constant fear of them? If you did, you would be a hypochondriac. The only appropriate response is to eat the right foods, get enough rest and exercise, and keep yourself and your possessions clean. Your immune system will protect you. However, if you didn't believe in germs, you'd be less likely to take those protective measures.

It's the same in the spiritual realm. Demons are like invisible germs looking for someone to infect. We are never told in Scripture to be afraid of them. You just need to be aware of their existence and commit yourself to knowing the truth and living a righteous life. The only real sanctuary you have is your position in Christ, and in Him, you have all the protection you need.

In Ephesians 6:10-18, Paul describes the armor of God, which He has provided for our protection. The first fact you should understand about God's protection is that our role is not passive. Notice how often we are commanded to take an active role:

> *Be strong* in the Lord and in the strength of His might. *Put on* the full armor of God, that you may

be able to *stand firm* against the schemes of the devil. For our struggle is not against flesh and blood, but against the rulers, against the powers, against the world forces of this darkness, against the spiritual forces of wickedness in the heavenly places. Therefore, *take up* the full armor of God, that you will *be able* to *resist* in the evil day, and having done everything, to *stand firm* (verses 10-13).

Some Christians ask, "If the Lord has disarmed the enemy and fitted me with armor, why can't I just trust in that?" That's like a person joining the military asking, "Our country has the most advanced tanks, planes, missiles, and ships in the world. Why should I go through basic training and learn how to stand guard?"

In her classic book *War on the Saints*, Jessie Penn-Lewis wrote, "The chief condition for the working of evil spirits in a human being, apart from sin, is passivity, in exact opposition to the condition which God requires from His children for His working in them."[6] You can't expect God to protect you from demonic influences if you don't take an active part in your own defense.

Our "commanding officer" has provided everything we need to remain victorious over the forces of darkness. He says, in effect, "I've prepared a winning strategy and designed effective equipment and weapons. But if you don't do your part by staying on active duty and learning

to use what I've given you, you're likely to become a casu-
alty of war."

Dressed for Battle

Because we are in an ongoing spiritual battle, Paul
chose to explain our protection in Christ by using the
imagery of armor:

> Stand firm therefore, having girded your loins
> with truth, and having put on the breastplate of
> righteousness, and having shod your feet with the
> preparation of the gospel of peace; in addition to
> all, taking up the shield of faith with which you
> will be able to extinguish all the flaming missiles of
> the evil one. And take the helmet of salvation, and
> the sword of the Spirit, which is the word of God
> (Ephesians 6:14-17).

When we put on the armor of God, we are putting
on the armor of light, which is the Lord Jesus Christ
(Romans 13:12-14). When we put on Christ, we take ourselves out of the realm of the flesh, where we are vulnera-
ble to attack, which is why we are instructed to "make no
provision for the flesh" (Romans 13:14). Satan has nothing in Christ (John 14:30), and to the extent that we put
on Christ, the evil one cannot touch us (1 John 5:18).

Armor You've Already Put On

It would appear from the verb tenses in Ephesians 6:14-15 that the first three pieces of the armor—belt, breastplate, and shoes—are already on you: "having girded," "having put on," "having shod." You strapped on those three pieces of armor the moment you received Jesus Christ as your Lord and Savior. The past tense of the verb, "having," signifies that the action it refers to was completed before we were instructed to stand firm. That's the logical way a soldier would prepare for action: he would make sure his protective armor is on before engaging the enemy.

The belt of truth. Jesus said, "I am...the truth" (John 14:6). Because Christ is in you, the truth is in you. The belt of truth is our defense against Satan's primary weapon, which is deception. "Whenever he [Satan] speaks a lie, he speaks from his own nature, for he is a liar and the father of lies" (John 8:44). You gird your loin with truth by standing firm in your faith.

Lying may be the number one social problem in America, and believing lies is what keeps people in bondage. Ironically, most people lie to protect themselves, but in reality, *truth* is our first line of defense. Truth is never an enemy—it is a liberating friend.

The only thing a Christian ever has to admit to is the truth. If a thought comes to mind that contradicts God's truth, dismiss it. If an opportunity comes along to say or do something that compromises or conflicts with truth, avoid it. Adopt a simple rule for living: If it's the truth, I'm in; if it's not the truth, count me out.

When Jesus was about to leave this planet and depart from the remaining disciples, He offered what is called the High Priestly Prayer, and it reveals His primary concern for the church: "I do not ask You to take them out of the world, but to keep them from the evil one" (John 17:15). How? "Sanctify them in the truth; Your Word is truth" (verse 17). You overcome the father of lies with divine revelation, not human reasoning or research.

The breastplate of righteousness. When you put on Christ at salvation, you are justified before our holy God (Romans 5:1)—not with *your* righteousness, but Christ's (1 Corinthians 1:30; Philippians 3:8-9). Putting on the breastplate of righteousness is your defense against the accuser. So when Satan aims an arrow at you by saying, "You're not good enough to be a Christian," you can respond, with Paul, "Who will bring a charge against God's elect? God is the one who justifies" (Romans 8:33).

Even though we stand on our righteous position in Christ, we should be aware of any deeds of unrighteousness. We are saints who sin. Putting on the armor of light means we walk in the light as He is in the light (1 John 1:6-8). Walking in the light is not sinless perfection. It means living in continuous agreement with God. "If we confess our sins, He is faithful and righteous to forgive

us our sins and to cleanse us from all unrighteousness"
(1 John 1:9).

Confession is not saying, "I'm sorry." It is saying "I
did it" the moment you sense the conviction of sin. Many
people are sorry, but usually they are sorry they got caught,
and even then they will only acknowledge as little as they
have to. To confess (Greek, *homologeo*) means to acknowledge or to agree. It is the same as walking in the light. Cov-
ering up anything is walking in darkness.

You can walk in the light because you're already forgiven. Why not be honest with God, who already knows
everything you have done and thought? Because of His
grace, your eternal destiny is not at stake when you sin,
but your daily victory is. Confession of sin clears the way
for the fruitful expression of righteousness in your daily
life. Follow Paul's example: "I also do my best to main-
tain always a blameless conscience both before God and
before men" (Acts 24:16).

The shoes of peace. When you receive Christ, you are
united with the Prince of Peace. "Having been justified
by faith, we have peace with God through our Lord Jesus
Christ" (Romans 5:1). "Let the peace of Christ rule in
your hearts." You do that by letting "the Word of Christ
richly dwell within you" (Colossians 3:15-16).

The shoes of peace become protection against the divi-
sive schemes of the devil when you act as a peacemaker
among believers (Romans 14:19). Peacemakers encourage

fellowship and have a ministry of reconciliation. Fellowship and unity in the body of Christ are based on our common spiritual heritage. True believers are children of God, and that's enough to bring us together in peace. If you are withholding fellowship with someone until you agree perfectly on every point of doctrine, you'll be the loneliest Christian on earth. We need to make a concerted effort to be "diligent to preserve the unity of the Spirit in the bond of peace" (Ephesians 4:3). "Blessed are the peacemakers, for they shall be called sons of God" (Matthew 5:9). Be assured that "the God of peace will soon crush Satan under your feet" (Romans 16:20).

The Rest of the Armor

Paul mentions three more pieces of armor that we must "take up" to protect ourselves from Satan's attack: the shield of faith, the helmet of salvation, and the sword of the Spirit, which is the Word of God. The first three are established by our position in Christ; the last three we "take up" to win daily battles.

The shield of faith. The object of our faith is God and His Word. The more you know about them, the more faith you will have. The less you know, the smaller your shield will be, and the easier it will be for one of Satan's fiery darts to reach its target. If you want your shield of faith to grow large and protective, your knowledge of God and His Word must increase (Romans 10:17).

These flaming missiles from Satan are nothing more than smoldering lies, burning accusations, and fiery temptations bombarding our minds. Whenever you discern a deceptive thought, accusation, or temptation, defuse it with truth. Jesus withstood Satan's temptation by quoting Scripture. Every time you memorize a Bible verse, listen to a good sermon, or participate in a Bible study, you enlarge your shield of faith.

The helmet of salvation. Every defeated Christian I have met with has doubted their salvation. Paul wrote in 1 Thessalonians 5:8, "Since we are of the day, let us be sober, having put on the breastplate of faith and love, and as a helmet, the hope of salvation." Salvation delivers us from the penalty of sin, but even more it protects us from the power of sin, and someday from the presence of sin. Without this hope, the Christian can easily be wounded in battle. In 2 Peter 1:4-11, we are told how to have the assurance of salvation:

> [Jesus our Lord] has granted to us His precious and magnificent promises, so that by them you may become partakers of the divine nature, having escaped the corruption that is in the world by lust. Now for this very reason also, applying all diligence, in your faith supply moral excellence, and in your moral excellence, knowledge, and in your knowledge, self-control, and in your self-control,

perseverance, and in your perseverance, godliness, and in your godliness, brotherly kindness, and your brotherly kindness, love. For if these qualities are yours and are increasing, they render you neither useless nor unfruitful in the true knowledge of our Lord Jesus Christ. For he who lacks these qualities is blind or short-sighted, having forgotten his purification from his former sins. Therefore, brethren, be all the more diligent to make certain about His calling and choosing you; for as long as you practice these things, you will never stumble; for in this way the entrance into the eternal kingdom of our Lord and Savior Jesus Christ will be abundantly supplied to you.

The sword of the Spirit. The Word of God is the only offensive weapon in the armor of God. Paul used *rhema* instead of *logos* for "word" in Ephesians 6:17 because he wanted to emphasize the spoken word of God. There is only one Word of God, but the Greek word *rhema* carries with it the idea of proclamation. (The emphasis of *logos* is more on the content.)

Our defense against direct attacks by the evil one is to speak aloud God's truth because Satan is not omniscient, and he doesn't perfectly know what you're thinking. By observing you, he can get a pretty good idea of what you are thinking, just as any student of human behavior can.

But he doesn't know what you're going to do before you do it. If you pay attention to a deceiving spirit (see 1 Timothy 4:1), he will know whether you believe his lie by how you behave. In addition, if he gave you the thought, then he will know what you are thinking.

You are ascribing too much power to Satan if you think he can read your mind perfectly and know the future perfectly. Occultic practices may attempt to read your mind or predict the future, but only God perfectly knows what is on your mind, and only He perfectly knows the future. You should never ascribe to Satan the divine attributes of God. The good news is you can communicate silently with God in your mind and carry on unspoken communion with your heavenly Father.

It should surprise no one that most spiritual attacks happen when you are alone, and usually at night. One of Job's friends had such an encounter:

> Now a word was brought to me stealthily; and my ear received a whisper of it. Amid disquieting thoughts from the visions of the night, when deep sleep falls on men, dread came upon me, and trembling, and made all my bones shake. Then a spirit passed by my face; the hair of my flesh bristled up. It stood still, but I could not discern its appearance; a form was before my eyes; there was silence, then I heard a voice: "Can mankind be just before

God? Can a man be pure before his Maker?" (Job 4:12-17).

"A word" was not a word from the Lord. God doesn't come to us "stealthily." That was a visit by the accuser of the brethren, who had a message for Job: *You are suffering because of your sin.* In truth, however, Job was suffering because "there is none like him on earth, a blameless and upright man, fearing God and turning away from evil" (Job 1:8).

Good people *do* suffer for the sake of righteousness. Christians all over the world are having demonic visitations at night, similar to that described in Job. Deep sleep is suddenly aroused by an overwhelming sense of fear that makes their hair stand up. Some report a sensation of pressure on their chest, and when they try to respond physically, they seemingly can't, as though something was grabbing their throats and holding them down. At such times, the presence of evil is all you sense, but God is also present.

Please don't assume that every time you awaken at night it is because you are under attack. You are probably waking up because of the pickle you ate, or a noise in the house, or just as a natural occurrence. However, if it does happen repeatedly at a precise time of night, it likely is a spiritual attack, and it's not necessarily because you're doing something wrong. You may be experiencing spiritual opposition because you are doing something *right*. In fact, if you are *not* experiencing some spiritual opposition to your ministry, there's a good chance that Satan doesn't see you as any threat to his plans.

At conferences, I have asked those in attendance: "How many of you have awakened suddenly at night with an overwhelming sense of fear at a precise time, like 3:00 a.m.?" I have never seen less than a third of the people raise their hands. At a conference for 250 leaders of a megachurch, 95 percent of the attendees raised their hands. When I first started doing a conference we called Resolving Personal and Spiritual Conflicts, I was attacked the night before every conference at 3:00 a.m., and this continued for four years, then stopped. I quickly learned how to stop the attacks and go back to sleep. If I did nothing, I would toss and turn until 4:00 a.m.

How do we call upon the name of the Lord and be saved if we can't speak? First, these encounters are not a physical battle that requires a physical effort on our part, because "the weapons of our warfare are not of the flesh, but divinely powerful for the destruction of fortresses" (2 Corinthians 10:4). Second, notice the order in which the following commands are stated: "Submit therefore to God. Resist the devil and he will flee from you" (James 4:7). You can always submit to God inwardly because He knows the thoughts and intentions of the heart (Hebrews 4:12). The moment you call upon His name, you will be free to verbally resist the devil. All you have to say is "Jesus," but you would have to say it. God may be allowing this in order to test your faith. Remembering this has certainly made me more dependent on Him.

Praying by the Spirit

After instructing us to put on the armor of God, Paul wrote, "With all prayer and petition, pray at all times in the Spirit, and with this in view, be on the alert with all perseverance and petition for all the saints" (Ephesians 6:18). "The Spirit also helps our weakness; for we do not know how to pray as we should, but the Spirit Himself intercedes for us" (Romans 8:26). This suggests the Holy Spirit comes alongside, picks us up, and takes us to the throne of grace. Any prayer that God the Holy Spirit prompts us to pray is a prayer that God our heavenly Father will always answer.

Combatting Spiritual Blindness

There are specific needs we should consider for prayer in spiritual warfare. One need relates to the blindness that Satan has inflicted on unbelievers (2 Corinthians 4:3-4). People cannot come to Christ unless their spiritual eyes are opened. Prayer is a primary weapon in combating spiritual blindness. The apostle John wrote, "If we ask anything according to His will, He hears us. And if we know that He hears us in whatever we ask, we know

that we have the requests which we have asked from Him"
(1 John 5:14-15). That assurance of answered prayer is fol-
lowed by the instruction for believers to ask God to bring
life to unbelievers (verse 16).

When the Holy Spirit lays concern for an unbeliever
on my heart, I always pray that God would send a mes-
senger to that person and that God would give that person
life. You can also pray that the eyes of lost people would
be opened to the truth that will set them free in Christ.

We can also pray as Paul did in Ephesians 1:18-19, that
the eyes of believers may be enlightened to understand
spiritual power, authority, and protection, which is their
inheritance in Christ. As long as Satan can keep us in the
dark about our position and authority in Christ, he can
keep us stunted in our growth and ineffectual in our witness and ministry. We need to pray for each other continually that Satan's smoke screen of lies will be blown away
and that our vision will be crystal clear.

Binding the Strong Man

Another purpose for authoritative prayer is binding
the "strong man" mentioned in Matthew 12:29. Jesus said,
"How can anyone enter the strong man's house and carry
off his property, unless he first binds the strong man?" He
was saying that you cannot rescue people from the bonds
of spiritual blindness or demonic influence unless you
first overpower their captors. Satan is disarmed, but he

will not let go of anything he thinks he can keep until we exercise the authority delegated to us by the Lord Jesus Christ. By faith we lay hold of the property in Satan's clutches that rightfully belongs to God, and we hold on until Satan turns loose.

C. Fred Dickason, who taught at Moody Bible Institute for years, gives several helpful suggestions for how to pray for someone who is being harassed by demons:[7]

1. Pray that the demons may be cut off from all communication and help from other demons and Satan.

2. Pray that the demons would be confused and weakened in their hold on the person.

3. Pray that the person would be strengthened in his faith to understand his position in Christ and to trust and obey God's Word.

4. Pray that the person may be able to distinguish between his thoughts and feelings and those of Satan.

5. Pray that the person might recognize the demonic presence and not be confused, but willingly seek godly counsel and help.

6. Pray that God would protect and guide His child and set angelic forces at work to break up every scheme of the enemy.

When I was on the staff of a large church, I entered the lunchroom one day and noticed a tall man in his mid-twenties alone at the other end of the room. He was a total stranger to any of us, and was standing at the chalkboard writing tiny words and then erasing them.

I said, "Hi, my name is Neil. Can I help you?"

"Oh, I don't know," he answered as he put down the chalk. He said his name was Bill. He looked and sounded like his mind had been blown by drugs, so I walked him outside to talk. He told me he worked at a local carwash, and I invited him to attend church. After an hour of conversation, he left.

A couple days later, Bill came back, and we talked more. Two weeks later, I was in my office when my intercom buzzed. "There's a guy down here named Bill who wants to see you."

"Send him up," I answered.

When he arrived, I got right to the point. "I'm glad you're here, Bill," I began. "May I ask you a personal question?" Bill nodded. "Have you ever trusted in Christ to be your Lord and your Savior?"

"No."

"Would you like to?"

"I don't know," Bill answered.

I reached for a salvation tract and read through it with him. "Do you understand this, Bill?"

"Yes."

"Would you like to make that decision for Christ right now?"

"Yes."

I wasn't sure he could read, so I said, "I'll pray a simple prayer of commitment, and you can repeat it after me phrase by phrase, okay?"

"Okay."

"Lord Jesus, I need You," I began.

Bill started to respond, "Lor-r-r..." Then he locked up completely. I could sense the oppression in the room.

"Bill, there's a battle going on for your mind," I said. "I'm going to read some Scripture and pray out loud for you. I'm going to bind the enemy and stand against him. As soon as you can, you just tell Jesus what you believe."

His eyes revealed that the battle was raging. After about 15 minutes of prayer and Scripture, Bill suddenly groaned, "Lord Jesus, I need You." Then he slumped back in his chair as if he had just completed ten rounds of a boxing match. He looked at me with tear-filled eyes and said, "I'm free." He knew it, and I could see it.

Understanding the spiritual nature of our world should have a profound effect on our evangelistic strategy. All too often we proclaim the virtues of Christianity to unbelievers as if we were standing outside a prison compound proclaiming to the inmates the benefits of living in the outside world. But unless someone overpowers the prison guards and opens the gates, how can the prisoners experience the freedom we're telling them about? We must learn to bind the strong man before we will be able to rescue his prisoners.

God has not only equipped you with everything you need to ward off the attack of the strong man, but He has also equipped you and authorized you for search and rescue in the lives of those who are in the devil's clutches. Stand firm in the armor that God has provided and step out in Christ's authority to plunder the strong man's house for God.

NOTES

1 Luther, *Table Talk*, IV, 5097, cited by Father Louis Coulange (pseud. Joseph Turmell), *The Life of the Devil* (London: Alfred A. Knopf, 1929), 147-148.

2 David Powlison, *Power Encounters: Reclaiming Spiritual Warfare* (Grand Rapids, MI: Baker, 1995), 135.

3 Thomas Brooks, *Precious Remedies Against Satan's Devices* (Carlisle, PA: Banner of Truth, 1984).

4 "The Steps to Freedom in Christ" is a repentance process that is included in my book *The Bondage Breaker* and at Freedom in Christ Ministries (www.ficm.org).

5 Neil T. Anderson, *Becoming a Disciple-Making Church* (Minneapolis, MN: Bethany House, 2016), 52-53.

6 Jessie Penn-Lewis, *War on the Saints*, 9th ed. (New York: Thomas E. Lowe, Ltd., 1973).

7 C. Fred Dickason, *Demon Possession and the Christian* (Chicago, IL: Moody Press, 1987), 255.

Go beyond this booklet...

Your Identity in Christ is excerpted from the bestseller *The Bondage Breaker®*, with more than 2 million copies sold worldwide.

In this significantly revised and updated edition, Neil offers a holistic approach to spiritual warfare that is rooted in the Word of God. As you read stories of others who have been locked in spiritual battles, you will learn the underlying whys and hows behind these attacks and discover the truths that set people free in Jesus.

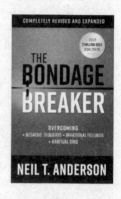

Dr. Neil T. Anderson is founder and president emeritus of Freedom in Christ Ministries, which has representation in more than 70 countries. Formerly a professor of practical theology at Talbot School of Theology, he is the author or co-author of 70 books.

You can find out more about these resources and Freedom in Christ Ministries at ficm.org